How I Feel

I Feel Bored

By Connor Stratton

level
2
little blue
readers

www.littlebluehousebooks.com

Little Blue House is distributed by North Star Editions:
sales@northstareditions.com | 888-417-0195

Produced for Little Blue House by Red Line Editorial.

Photographs ©: Shutterstock Images, cover, 4, 10–11, 12, 15 (top), 15 (bottom), 16–17, 18; iStockphoto, 6–7, 9 (top), 9 (bottom), 21, 23 (top), 23 (bottom), 24 (top left), 24 (top right), 24 (bottom left), 24 (bottom right)

Library of Congress Control Number: 2020913841

ISBN
978-1-64619-295-3 (hardcover)
978-1-64619-313-4 (paperback)
978-1-64619-349-3 (ebook pdf)
978-1-64619-331-8 (hosted ebook)

Printed in the United States of America
Mankato, MN
012021

About the Author

Connor Stratton enjoys writing books for children and watching movies, such as *Inside Out*. He's always trying to understand his feelings better. He lives in Minnesota.

Table of Contents

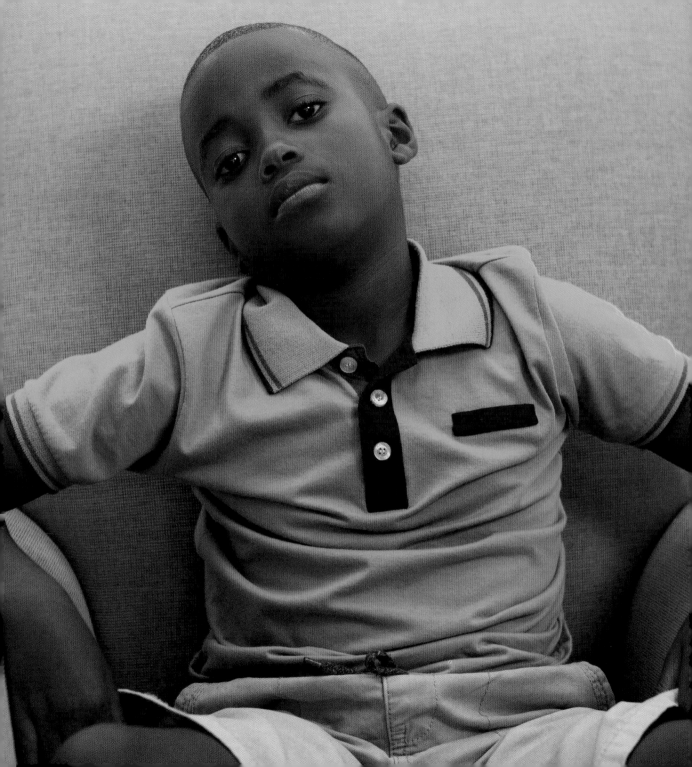

Finding Others

Sometimes there are no kids to play with at home. When that happens, I feel bored.

My friends come over, and we play outside.
My friends are fun, and I feel better.

friends

Sometimes it rains all day.

When I can't play outside,

I feel bored.

My sister and I play with toys inside.
Playing with my sister is fun.

By Myself

Sometimes I don't know what to do by myself.

Then I feel bored.

My parents can't play with me, and my sister can't play with me.

I have to play by myself.

I see paper and markers.
I draw a picture, and I
feel better.

marker

paper

On the Road

My family takes a trip
by car.

The trip takes a long time.

It's hard to wait in
my seat.
I want to do something,
but it feels like there is
nothing to do.
I feel bored.

I make up a game.

I try to find red things.

The sign is red, and that man's hat is red.

The game is fun, and I'm not bored anymore.

Glossary

car

seat

markers

sign

Index